CONTENTS

All words in **bold** appear in the glossary on page 30.

WHAT ARE FAIRIES?

Fairies are magical creatures. Most people think that they are imaginary, but others believe that they really do exist.

Most people have never seen a real fairy. Stories say that you will only ever see fairies, like this one, if you believe in them. Do you believe in fairies?

If you believe in fairies and you know where to look, perhaps you will catch a peek of these tiny folk. Look in their favourite places, such as bluebell woods and flower gardens (right).

IT'S AMAZING!

Some people think that cats can see fairies and other magical creatures that humans cannot.

WHAT DO FAIRIES LOOK LIKE?

You can't take real photographs of fairies, so some people draw pictures of them from their imagination. Others create photographs of fairies, like this one.

Fairies usually look like tiny people. Most have wings and many have a magical glow around them.

If you see a little bright light hovering in the air, look closely at it. It might be a fairy!

Fairies love flowers, and some make beautiful clothes from flower petals. One petal might be enough to make a whole fairy dress! Other fairies use leaves and tree bark to make their outfits.

Fairy royalty

Fairy kings and queens (left) are the most beautiful fairies of all. They are also more magical than normal fairies!

FAIRYLAND

Fairies live in secret places that are hidden away from humans. Here fairies dance and play with all sorts of creatures. These secret realms are known as fairylands (below).

Fairylands can be hidden under hills, under lakes, in forests or on islands that can disappear.

IT'S AMAZING!
FAIRIES

Annabel Savery

523 291 32 2

Franklin Watts
Published in Great Britain in 2016 by The Watts Publishing Group

Copyright © The Watts Publishing Group 2011

All rights reserved.

Planning and production by Discovery Books Limited
Managing Editor: Laura Durman
Editor: Annabel Savery
Designer: Ian Winton

Picture credits: Alamy: p. 10 (Tim Gartside), p. 12 (Mary Evans Picture Library), p. 14 &
p. 15 top & p. 24 & p. 26 (all AF archive), p. 16 (Moviestore collection Ltd); Getty Images:
p. 7 bottom (C. Wilhelm), p. 8 (Nostalgia), p. 18 (Richard Doyle), p. 28 (SSPL via Getty
Images); GirlGuidingUK: p. 23 bottom; Library of Congress: p. 29 top; Photoshot: p. 27; Rex
Features: p. 25 (Alastair Muir), p. 29 bottom (Everett Collection); Shutterstock Images:
title page (Liliya Kulianionak), p. 4 (Algol), p. 5 top (Keepsmiling4u), p. 5 bottom (Tony
Campbell), p. 6 (Miroslava Vasileva Arnaudova), p. 7 top & p. 30 (greglith), p. 9 main
(Hannamariah), p. 9 inset & p. 31 (greglith), p. 9 bottom (Tompet), p. 11 top (_EG_), p. 11
bottom (RLN), p. 13 top (Liliya Kulianionak), p. 13 bottom left (Robyn Mackenzie), p. 13
bottom right (TRE Wheeler BA (Hons)), p. 15 bottom (Pushkin), p. 17 top (marymary),
p. 17 bottom (Scorpp), p. 19 top (graph), p. 19 bottom (Julien Tromeur), p. 20 left (Shipov
Oleg), p. 20 right (lenetstan), p. 21 top (Chas), p. 22 top (Algol), p. 22 bottom & p. 23 top
(both Andreas Meyer); WikiMedia Commons: p. 21 bottom.

Cover: Main (Shutterstock Images: greglith) & background (iStockPhoto.com: digital_eye)

Every attempt has been made to clear copyright. Should there be any
inadvertent omission, please apply to the publisher for rectification.

Dewey number: 398.2′1
ISBN: 978 1 4451 4984 4

Franklin Watts
An imprint of
Hachette Children's Group
Part of The Watts Publishing Group
Carmelite House
50 Victoria Embankment
London EC4Y 0DZ

An Hachette UK company
www.hachette.co.uk

www.franklinwatts.co.uk

Fairylands have secret, magical entrances that only fairies can find. Humans cannot enter fairyland unless they have a fairy guide. Some people believe that primroses (left) can unlock the secret doors to fairyland.

Stuck in fairyland

You might think it would be wonderful to visit fairyland. But beware – if you eat or drink anything in fairyland you will be stuck there forever!

FAIRY MAGIC

Fairies can do all kinds of magic – good and bad!

Fairies cast spells with a wave of their magic wands (above) or a sprinkle of fairy dust. They can use their magic to help humans or to put spells on them.

Fairies can **disguise** themselves as anything they choose. A fairy might look like a little old man or the most beautiful lady – you never know!

There are ways to spot a fairy in disguise, though. Look out for people with very pointy ears (right) and feet that are back to front.

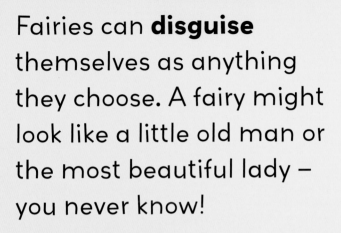

Fairy music

Fairies love to play music. If humans hear it, they can spend years listening, but believe that only a day has passed.

FAIRY FUN

Most of all, fairies like to have fun.

Fairies love to dance and make music. When there is a full moon, all fairies come out to dance and play in the moonlight. They have wonderful feasts and parties.

Fairies often dance in a special place called a fairy ring. You might have seen one — to us it looks like a small circle of toadstools.

Fairies are good friends with all the animals. Sometimes fairies ride on the backs of insects such as dragonflies, butterflies and grasshoppers.

Bluebells

Bluebells are magical flowers. The ringing of bluebells in the woods calls the fairies out to play.

GOOD FAIRIES

Fairy godmothers are protective magical beings. They watch over young girls, especially princesses, to make sure no harm comes to them.

The most famous fairy godmother is a **character** in the fairytale *Cinderella* (right). Cinderella is helped by her fairy godmother. She sends Cinderella to the ball where she meets Prince Charming.

Not so nice!

In the film *Shrek 2* there is a rather different fairy godmother. She is very mean and only interested in helping her son, Prince Charming!

The tooth fairy (left) is a good fairy. When your baby teeth fall out, you should leave them under your pillow. The tooth fairy will visit in the night and change each tooth for a coin!

BAD FAIRIES

Not all fairies are good though – some are very bad! Bad fairies can cause lots of trouble.

In the fairytale *Sleeping Beauty* a wicked fairy becomes angry when she is not invited to a princess's **christening**. She casts an evil spell so that when the princess grows up she will prick her finger on a spinning wheel (right) and die.

Good fairies change the spell so that the princess will sleep for a hundred years instead.

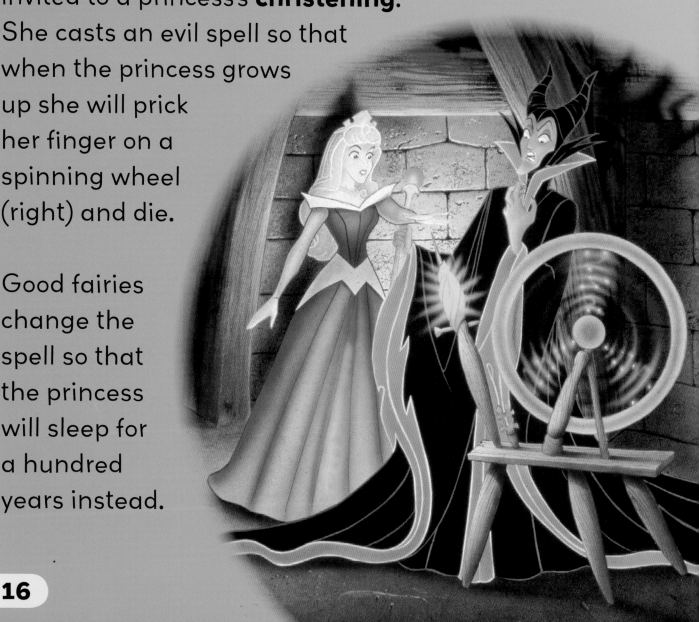

Rumpelstiltskin

Rumpelstiltskin is a **manikin** fairy from a story by the Brothers Grimm. He spins gold from straw to help a young girl, but he asks for the girl's first child in return!

In Scottish **folklore** all fairies are **mischievous**, but some are really mean. Scottish people leave gifts of butter, cream or cake out for fairies to try to keep them from causing harm.

FAIRIES AROUND THE WORLD

Around the world there are many different fairy beliefs.

In Ireland fairies are called 'sidhe'. They are believed to be an ancient race of gods that have become smaller and smaller. They can only be seen by humans on **Midsummer's Eve** (above).

A Japanese fairy creature is the Blossom Princess called 'Konohana-Sakuya Hime'. It is the **spirit** of the cherry tree (below).
Stories warn people never to cut a branch from the cherry tree or the spirit will die.

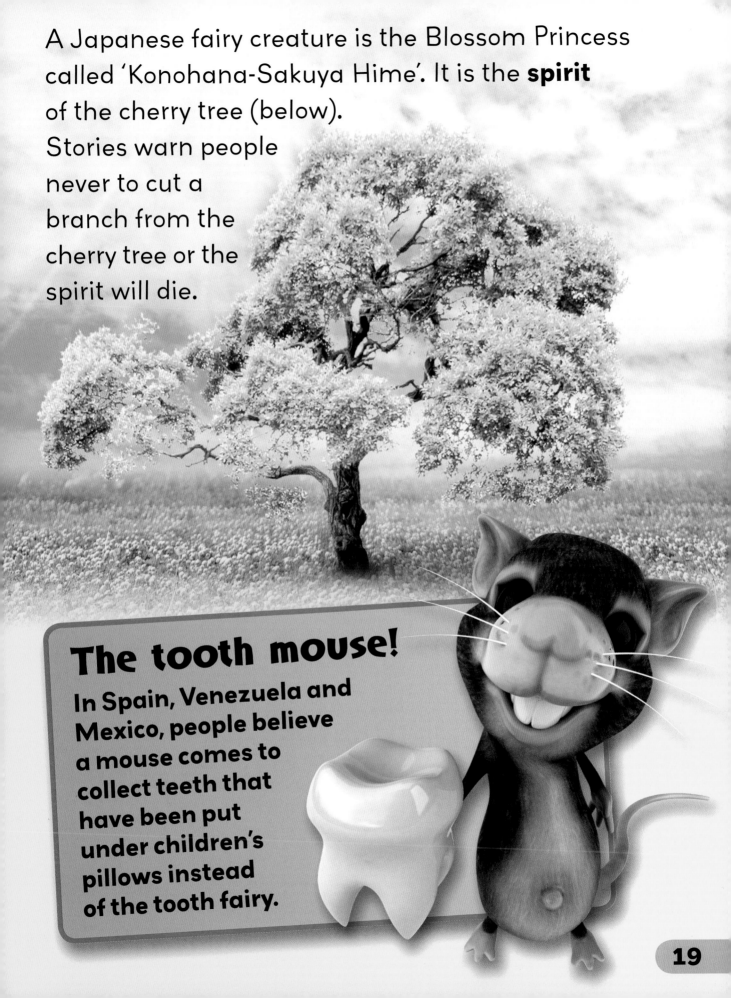

The tooth mouse!

In Spain, Venezuela and Mexico, people believe a mouse comes to collect teeth that have been put under children's pillows instead of the tooth fairy.

SUPERSTITIONS

A superstition is something that people believe, but it might or might not be true. There are all sorts of superstitions about fairies.

Some people think that if you don't clap your hands after sneezing, fairies will die.

Other people believe that it is unlucky to say the word 'fairy'. They think that if you say the word, it calls fairies to come to you. If you do not need the fairies they will be cross, and cause you bad luck.

A four-leaf clover is a lucky find, and some people think that if you wear one you'll be able to see fairies.

Changelings!

Some fairies are believed to steal human babies and replace them with fairy babies. These babies are called changelings. They might have green skin or eyes!

Many magical creatures are types of fairies.

Elves, sprites and pixies are all types of fairies. Elves (left) are beautiful creatures with great magic. Sprites are fairies that are the spirits of things in nature, such as water, rainbows or flowers.

Pixies (right) are thought to be naughty, often misleading travellers so that they get lost.

Goblins (right) are strange creatures that live in your house and make noise at night. They give presents to children who are good – but play tricks on those who are naughty.

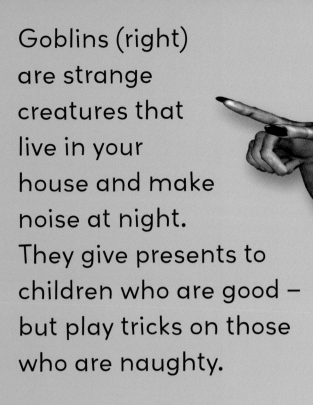

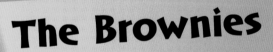

The Brownies

Brownies are small, helpful fairies. They look after your home and clean and tidy during the night. This is where the girl guide group, the Brownies, get their name from. They promise to do a good deed every day – without being asked!

FAIRY CHARACTERS

Some of the best-loved fairies are characters in stories, plays, musicals and even ballets.

William Shakespeare uses several fairy characters in his plays. These include Oberon and Titania (above) – the king and queen of the fairies, the mischievous elf Puck and Ariel the storm fairy.

Fairytales

You might think that fairytales would always contain fairy characters. The name 'fairytale' originally comes from old tales about fairies and their lands. Now it is used for lots of stories about magical lands and creatures.

In the ballet *The Nutcracker* (below) the Sugar Plum Fairy welcomes Clara to the Kingdom of Sweets with a beautiful dance. Clara is enchanted by the fairy's beauty.

FAIRIES IN FILMS

How many famous fairy film stars can you think of? Here are some to get you started!

Tinker Bell is probably the best-known fairy. She appears in films such as *Peter Pan* and *Hook*. Disney have even created Tinker Bell films. These are set in Pixie Hollow, the land of the fairies.

Tinker Bell

Tinker Bell was invented by J.M. Barrie in his story, *Peter Pan*. Tinker Bell is Peter Pan's helpful friend, but she gets very jealous when he becomes friends with Wendy – a girl from the real world.

Thumbelina (below) appears in a fairytale by Hans Christian Andersen. She is only the size of a thumb and grows from a **barleycorn.**

When tiny Thumbelina meets her true love, a flower-fairy prince, she is given a pair of wings to match his. This means they can fly from flower to flower together.

ARE FAIRIES REAL?

Some people believe that fairies are real – but is there any proof?

Between 1917 and 1922 two girls took photos of themselves with fairies near their home in Cottingley, UK (below). The photos were printed in newspapers and soon everyone was talking about them.

Many people believed that the pictures were real – even some scientists.

IT'S AMAZING!

One of the most famous people to believe the girls' story was Sir Arthur Conan Doyle, author of the *Sherlock Holmes* stories.

Most people now believe that the photos were fake, but the girls never admitted that they were, even when they were old ladies. Later, a film was made of the girls' story. It's called *FairyTale: A True Story* (below).

Whether you believe that fairies are real or not, they are very magical creatures!

GLOSSARY

barleycorn the seed of a barley plant

character a person in a story, play or film

christening a Christian religious ceremony at which a baby is given a name

disguise to change the way you look so that you are not recognised

exist to live or be real

folklore the stories and traditions of a group of people from a certain place or country

imaginary existing only in the imagination

manikin a very small man with magical powers

Midsummer's Eve an evening in the middle of summer, in June, that is celebrated in many countries

mischievous behaving in a naughty or teasing way

protective keeping someone or something safe from harm

realm a kingdom

spirit a being that is not of this world

superstition a belief that may or may not be true

FURTHER INFORMATION

Books

Fairies and Magical Creatures (Encyclopedia Mythologica), Matthew Reinhart
    & Robert Sabuda, Walker.

How to Find Flower Fairies, Cicely Mary Barker, Warne.

Dressing Up as a Fairy, Rebekah Shirley, Franklin Watts.

Rainbow Magic Series, Daisy Meadows, Orchard Books.

Websites

Play games and create your own fairy at the Disney Fairies website.
    http://disney.co.uk/disney-fairies/

This website contains pictures of and information about the flower fairies by
    author Cicely Mary Barker.
    www.flowerfairies.com/UK/home.html

Read all sorts of stories about fairies and other magical creatures at
    Long, Long Time Ago.
    www.longlongtimeago.com/once-upon-a-time/fairytales/

Films

A Midsummer Night's Dream, 20th Century Fox
    Home Entertainment, 1999.

Cinderella, Walt Disney Home Video, 1950.

FairyTale – A True Story, Warner Home
    Video, 1998.

Peter Pan, Walt Disney Studios Home
    Entertainment, 1953.

Sleeping Beauty, Disney, 1958.

Thumbelina, 20th Century Fox Home
    Entertainment, 1994.

Tinker Bell and The Great Fairy Rescue,
    Walt Disney Home Entertainment, 2010.

INDEX

Note to parents and teachers: Every effort has been made by the Publishers to ensure that the websites on page 31 are suitable for children, that they are of the highest educational value, and that they contain no inappropriate or offensive material. However, because of the nature of the Internet, it is impossible to guarantee that the contents of these sites will not be altered. We strongly advise that Internet access is supervised by a responsible adult.